Life Wisdom

Life
Wisdom

Carolyn Temsi

∽ AND ∽

Caro Handley

Hodder & Stoughton

First published in Great Britain in 2000 by Hodder and Stoughton
A division of Hodder Headline

A Hodder & Stoughton paperback

10 9 8 7 6 5 4 3

A CIP catalogue record for this title is available from the British Library

ISBN 0 340 76550 X

Typeset by Palimpsest Book Production Limited,
Polmont, Stirlingshire
Printed and bound in Great Britain by
Mackays of Chatham PLC, Chatham, Kent

Hodder and Stoughton
A division of Hodder Headline
338 Euston Road
London NW1 3BH

For Luke, my precious son, with endless love and deep gratitude, your Mum Carolyn.

For Jess, Claire and Matteo, with all my love Caro.

Our Story

We're best friends who met when we were both hard-working single mums. Carolyn was a marketing consultant running her own business and Caro was a journalist writing for women's magazines. We met through a mutual interest in humanistic psychotherapy. Both of us were combining our work with bringing up a young child alone, and we also found we had a great deal of other issues in common.

On the surface, our lives seemed great. We both had lovely children, successful careers, owned our own homes, had plenty of friends and interests. However, below this facade of having got it right lurked a whole number of issues that needed addressing. We wanted to settle down with lovely partners and have more children. We wanted to change careers and sort out our finances. We wanted less stress and conflict in our lives, plus better health and contentment.

Day by day, life threw up endless puzzles and challenges and we realised that we were not as free in our choices as we thought we were. We had unresolved baggage from the past and a set of habits and coping strategies that impacted upon the way we lived and got in the way of us getting what we truly wanted. Together we made a commitment to change this.

We were determined to understand the emotional, spiritual and psychological aspects of life as well as the practical skills. We wanted to make sure that we enjoyed the way that we lived, that we balanced our lives more effectively and that we created lives that we could be proud of.

The more we got to know ourselves, the more we realised just how much we could steer ourselves in the direction that we wanted. Gradually we began to understand where our responsibilities lay in all of this and how we could make changes in our lives which would result in real and lasting benefits.

The lessons along the way were tough, challenging, exciting and frustrating but always enriching. We helped ourselves and each other and developed a totally new understanding of life – this book is the result of what we have learnt and continue to practise.

We have written this book for ourselves, our partners, our children and for you. We hope that our wisdom enriches your journey to building the life that you want for yourself, and that it is one that is filled with peace, joy and satisfaction.

Introduction

We believe that there is nothing that you can't resolve, and that what you want in life can be yours.

We believe that this is your right.

Life Wisdom is here to guide and advise you, whether you're happy with the way that your life is going right now or you're facing difficulties.

Whether you are just starting out in life, need to know where to go from here, are struggling with something specific or want advice on day-to-day issues, *Life Wisdom* will answer your questions and set you on the path towards a truly interesting and satisfying life.

We have used the wisdom in this book to create happy, harmonious and fulfilling lives. We want to share this wisdom with as many people as possible, so that you too may experience the satisfaction and success in life that you deserve.

We wish you well.

How to use this book

Here is some guidance on how to form your question:

keep it simple;
ask for guidance and advice about your question
rather than for yes/no answers;
ask only what you are willing to have answered.

If you want *Life Wisdom* to help you, it means:
treating it with care and respect;
taking your time rather than rushing;
being willing to accept the advice offered;
opening yourself up to the possibility of change;
actively engaging in whatever is required of you;
accepting the answers, whatever they may be.

If you want a more detailed answer, open the book three
times while thinking of your question:
the first page will refer to the present moment;
the second to the immediate future;
the third to the long-term future.

Rhythms

When you open this book here, it is to remind you of the rhythms of life and the importance of going with rather than against them. Life moves in ways which are perfectly balanced, in and out, back and forth, one way and then the other. Nature reflects this, with the tides of the sea, day and night, the seasons of the year. After darkness comes the light, after scarcity comes abundance. In everything there is an ebb and flow, a pulsation, which gives us a model on which to base the way we live.

These rhythms appear in our lives, just as surely as they appear all around us. The pace at which you move forward towards a person or a goal is the pace at which you will then move away from it. If you are wildly enthusiastic about something, you may soon feel just as powerfully negative about it. If you move forward gently and thoughtfully you will back away gently too. Thus the less dramatically we approach something or someone, the less dramatically we will move away. If you wish to accomplish something specific, it is important to work with life's rhythms. Pick your timing, pick your pace and maximise your effect.

We are often puzzled by the way we can feel intensely close to someone and then need to back away from them for a period of time, however brief. Yet this is a natural rhythm – we can't stay intensely close all the time, just as we can't stay passionate about a task, an event or a goal indefinitely. Our feelings will come and go and all we have to do is trust in the process.

Eventually everything comes full circle. Our intensity and enthusiasm will come back, with the same focus, or sometimes with a different one.

Trust the process you are going through and know that whatever you are feeling right now is fine. Give yourself time, you don't have to take action this minute. Relax, breathe deeply, know that there is a bigger picture that you can't see right now. Whether you are in the ebb or the flow, know that you will feel the opposite pull sooner or later and all you have to do is to go with it, calmly and clearly.

Watch the rhythms of life and let them show you that everything happens in a perfect way.

Detach From The Outcome

When you open this book here, it is time to release yourself and let go of your attachment to a specific outcome. It is time instead to focus on the process rather than the end-result.

It's easy to get caught up in believing that you know what should happen, how people should behave and how things should turn out.

Are you desperately trying to control something or someone right now? Are you fearful as to what might happen if you were simply to let things unfold as they will?

If things are really stressful it's a sure sign that you are desperately avoiding taking your hands off a particular problem because you cannot foresee how things will turn out if you do let go. You go on and on managing it all in more ridiculous and exhausting ways because this seems less scary than what might happen if you were to stop. Your fear of the unknown keeps you hooked into the known, no matter how awful or distressing it may be. Or perhaps you have a clear idea of what you believe will happen and you feel that you can't bear to let that unfold.

Remember that you can't see into the future, know the whole picture or bring sufficient detachment to bear. You only have your limited perspective to base your desires upon. In this way you exclude the guiding hand of the universal forces which are acting to steer you on to your best path. However, if you let go of the specifics, you can trust that everything will be as it should be. Put your energy into desiring the best outcome for your overall well-being and happiness, for then you come in line with the universe and together you form a most powerful team.

Often fear of a negative outcome draws exactly what we most fear towards us. Have you been dwelling on a worst-case scenario? Are you fearing and preparing for what you don't want to happen? Well, now is the time to stop. Focus on the process. Put your energy into the journey rather than dissipating it with fears of where this journey will take you. It will take you wherever you are meant to be and the more you trust in that and fully experience the present moment, the more you will find that you like where you end up.

Know that the best Samurai was the one who concentrated on the fight and did not waste energy on whether he would win or lose. Such a strategy meant that he could give his all and invariably he would win. You can too. Detach now.

Emotions

When you open this book here, it is time to open up and let yourself feel your emotions. Whatever the issue in your life at the moment, know that it is simply reflecting what's going on in your emotions and when you deal with this you will move on from this issue.

Right now you are trying to avoid painful feelings. Unfortunately, stuffing painful feelings out of sight won't make them go away. They're bubbling below the surface, desperate to get out. And avoiding them makes it impossible to feel positive feelings in the way that you want to.

We push down our feelings because most of us have been brought up to believe that there are emotions which are unacceptable. Some of us learned that all emotions are unacceptable, others learned that specific emotions such as anger or tears are unacceptable. Still others learned to let their emotions pour out without any sense of what is appropriate. Whichever end of the scale you are on, the challenge is to find a balance where you acknowledge and experience your emotions in a safe, honest and responsible manner.

The good news is there's absolutely nothing wrong with any kind of feeling. It's avoiding feelings that hurts. Whatever you feel is OK, no matter what you were taught as a child. While some ways of behaving when experiencing feelings can be inappropriate, your feelings themselves can't be. In fact, you have no control over what you feel. When someone tells you not to feel sad or angry they're asking the impossible. You can deny the feelings you're having but you can't stop them from coming. So stop trying not to feel and celebrate the fact that you do. All feelings need in order to pass is to be acknowledged and accepted. Just saying to yourself, or someone else, 'I feel angry' (or sad, or frightened) is a great start. Let yourself have the feelings, accept that they can be uncomfortable and that you don't know how long they'll last. Cry, punch a pillow, get into bed, walk in the park, do whatever comforts you best while you feel this way.

When you deal with negative feelings you'll also be able to feel your positive feelings more fully, because the effort involved in not feeling our bad feelings carries over to our good feelings and keeps those away too. When you accept and respect all of your feelings you will be able to be who you truly are. Free yourself and feel all that life has to offer you.

Do Something Different

When you open this book here, know that it is time to stop repeating old behaviours and do something different. You're putting effort and energy into trying to get what you want in ways that don't work and it's leaving you frustrated and stuck.

What is it in your life that isn't working? What is it that you are struggling with? What is leaving you feeling exhausted, mentally or physically? Are you coming up against a brick wall and still pushing forward in the hope of knocking it down? Are you trying to solve a situation by tackling it in the same old way that's already failed many times? Do you find that no matter how hard you try, you end up back where you started?

Know that life is not meant to be a struggle. If something doesn't flow smoothly, if your efforts are not rewarded, then you need to stop what you are doing and try something different. Don't worry if you don't know what the something different is, the first step is just to stop the old behaviours. Trust that there is always something different to be tried, no matter how limited the options may seem. Don't wrack your brains for what to do – understanding that life is not about struggle means learning to let things come to you, simply and easily. Let the universal intelligence be your guide. If you stop what isn't working, then a solution will present itself and the way forward will become clear. It may take an hour, a day or months, but it will come. Or it may be that you already know what you need to try and you simply need to give yourself permission to go ahead. Be brave. Stopping the struggle will bring you relief and release energy which you can use in better ways.

Sometimes we're more attached to the struggle than to achieving the best outcome. If this is what is going on understand that the struggle is doing you no good. Let go of obstinacy. If you've been using aggressive tactics, be willing to soften. If you've been playing the victim, be willing to become active and to stand firm about who you are and what you want. When you do something different others will react differently too. Stop the struggle and know that there is always another way.

Courage

You have opened this book here to focus on one of life's most wonderful qualities. Courage is the power or quality which we use when facing adversity in life.

Are you going through a difficult time right now? Are you struggling with difficult events, circumstances or people? What are you dealing with that is stretching you to your limits? Or does it feel as though you're being stretched beyond them?

Well, now is the time to sit down, have a cry, a cup of tea — or both — and know that help is at hand. We are never alone and courage is what teaches us this. Each of us is filled with the ability to be courageous because courage is literally the simple act of tapping into the God force which is available to us all. This is what allows us and enables us to overcome our fears. It is connecting with the universal energy which surrounds us and protects us. It doesn't make us immortal or infallible but it does allow us to face fear, danger or pain with an inner strength which is always there when we look for it. Calm yourself and go inside and you will feel your courage there waiting for you. It won't always allay your fears or feelings but it will give you the strength to continue despite them.

You really can do it.

It may be that right now you need to have the courage of your convictions. To do whatever it is that you know to be right for you. To act in accordance with your own beliefs and to stand up and be counted. You may only manage to do this in a small way to begin with, but from there your courage will grow.

Don't ever criticise yourself or put yourself down for not having enough courage. Know that it takes courage just to be brave enough to question how courageous you are. If you are doing even this then you are courageous and, as we all know, from small acorns, huge oak trees grow.

Let your courage build, nurture yourself and all will be well.

Find The Child
In You

When you open this book here, it asks you to do something which is rarely given adequate importance. You need to find the child within you and befriend it.

We all carry with us our experience of being a child, even though it is often locked away, papered over and long forgotten. The child within you is the essence of your true soul. Innocent, pure, vulnerable, honest, intuitive, joyful and wise. This may not be how you experienced yourself as a child, or how others made you feel, but this is always who we all are under the layers of adaptation and distortion. Now is the time to uncover your specialness and reconnect with the child that you once were. And it is also the time to uncover your childhood experiences and pains.

When you do this you will realise how much of what has been going on for you is actually about the needs, concerns and vulnerabilities of this inner part of you. Have you been wondering where your reactions come from when they just don't seem to make sense? Are you confused by insecurities and neediness which just don't seem to fit with the adult version of yourself? Or are you so cut off from your inner child that you exist entirely within your rational adult part and cannot understand why life feels sterile and joyless? It is your inner child who will show you how to feel true joy and pleasure and to laugh and have fun.

Whatever your issue is now, know that it is tied up with the child within you. This part of you has the answers to your puzzles and will give you insights about the right decisions and the direction to take. Get to know it. Treat yourself with the softness and kindness that a young child warrants. Cuddle up in a blanket by the fire, buy some crayons, go to the park — listen to what it has to say. Buy a book on the inner child and embark upon or further your relationship with this part of yourself.

Know that there are different times when it is appropriate for the adult or the child parts of you to dominate, and that the child part only keeps interfering in adult issues when it isn't getting its needs met separately. These are the needs which weren't met by others when you were a child, but which you can meet now for yourself. And it's not just a question of giving to your inner child, for the child inside has a lot to give you in return. Get to know this child and let its sense of fun and joy into your life. Heal yourself, parent yourself in the ways you need, and gradually you'll experience the child in you flourishing into an essential ally.

Perfection

When you open this book here, it is because the notion of perfection is getting in the way for you right now.

When something is perfect it means that it is the best that it can be. That it is faultless and totally true to itself. We talk of a perfect square or a perfect right angle. A perfect right angle measures ninety degrees, not ninety-one and not eighty-nine. But trouble arises because we imagine we can transfer this concept of exactness on to our lives, other people and human nature. This can't be done. In life there is no exact measurement for what is right. We are not statistics or geometry.

In human terms, perfection is about being imperfect. It's about being the best that we can be, not the best that we could be if we were robots or some fantasised ideal that takes the humanity out of us, that removes our flaws, our foibles and our emotions and allows us to be like the characters in a story or a movie. Life is about balance. When we strive for perfection in one area, we compromise in another. The athlete who trains for hours every day has to sacrifice a great deal. The ballerina who can perform the perfect movement doesn't have perfect feet. They show the wear and tear of this commitment.

Stop and ask yourself what it is that you want to be perfect and where you got the notion that it could be? Real life isn't like our dreams or the fairy tales of childhood and that is what makes it rich and wonderful. If everything was perfect, how would we grow? How would you appreciate the good if you didn't experience the bad?

When you try too hard to control everything and make it perfect, it's a sure sign that you want to get away from reality and that you have feelings you are avoiding. There's nothing wrong with having high standards. There's nothing wrong with ambition and trying to get things right. But when you make getting what you want the only priority, it won't work. Now it is time to think again, to take a different approach, to moderate your needs and demands. To be more realistic.

It's OK to have weakness, to be unpredictable, to make mistakes, to have room for improvement, to misunderstand and do all the other things which make us human in our lives. The issue is keeping the balance so that neither these nor the search for perfection make our lives unhappy or unmanageable.

In fact, all is already perfectly imperfect, because everything always is exactly as it should be, in order for your life to unfold as it should.

Instinct

When you open this book here, it is to let you know that the most important thing you can do right now is to trust yourself and your own instincts. It is time to believe that you know what is right for you and what you need to do.

We all have instincts — the unconscious urges or impulses to respond or behave in a particular way which we have no way of explaining, other than that it feels right.

Too often instincts are ignored. We live in an age where we are told that if something is not scientifically proven then it has no value. Yet we all know that this is not true. Everyone has had occasions when they have simply known something without being told, or where they have responded instinctively to a situation, knowing that it was the right thing to do.

Think back to a time that this has happened to you in the past and know that the skill you showed then is available to you all the time. Reach inside yourself for the wonderful power of knowledge which you hold. You already know what to do in any situation and the best way to respond to anything that happens. All you have to do is to trust the wise, calm inner you, no matter what is going on around you or what others say.

So put aside those who judge and advise, forget statistics and information, walk away from well-meaning people who interfere. These are not what you need now. Instead, you have what you need in your own heart.

To make contact with your instinctive self, take some time out, relax and breathe deeply. Imagine journeying deep inside yourself and meeting the wise part of you who knows just what to do. Ask for advice and then bring back what you have learned and see how it applies to the situation you are in. Use what you discover with respect and care for yourself and others. And remember to keep on doing this as you deal with whatever it is you are going through. Your instincts can take you from start to finish. They will see you through the entire process if you let them.

Your instinct is a valuable ally. Don't dismiss or ignore it. Listen to what it tells you and you will reap the benefits.

The World Is
A Mirror

When you open this book here, it is because you need to know that you are projecting your thoughts, feelings and actions on to those around you. This means that although you may believe it has nothing to do with you, in fact what you see in others is a reflection of what is going on in you. The world around you operates just like a mirror, reflecting back to you behaviours, qualities, feelings and issues which are within you.

The trouble is, that because this process is largely unconscious, we end up mistakenly believing that what is outside us is nothing to do with us and that the emotions, behaviours and characteristics which we encounter in the world belong only to those who demonstrate them. We miss the way it informs us about ourselves.

What is the world presenting to you at the moment? Can you recognise that this is actually your feeling or issue, either superimposed on to another person or conveniently acted out by someone or something that bears exactly the characteristics that you need to address in yourself?

The fact that the world is a mirror is something that you need to learn about and become conscious of. For the ghosts of our inner selves haunt us and show themselves in others around us when we do not address them directly. Look at what is around you and recognise it as being yours, no matter how alien it is to you. If you find peace and joy filling your life, know that these qualities are within and that you are sending them out into your world. If there is angst, anger, difficulties, dishonesty or selfishness, know that these too come from within and are only reflected back to you by others, or through events, for you to acknowledge them as yours.

It is important to understand the connection between our outer and inner worlds because it is always the inner world we need to attend to and heal, in order to bring resolution to the outer world. As soon as you own an experience or a feeling which is being mirrored for you in the outside world, you will know the relief of being more connected to your true self. When you realise that you are only surrounded by angry or untrustworthy people because you hold that quality hidden within yourself, then you become empowered to deal with it consciously. And when you do this, the need to project such qualities diminishes and you can become truly free.

And remember when at other times you see qualities you like in the outside world, this is also yourself being mirrored back at you. You really are that wonderful. Everything in your life really is all about you.

Goodwill

When you open this book here, it is time to find your goodwill and bring it to whatever is going on in your life right now. Goodwill is a feeling of kindness, friendliness, cheerfulness and openness and it is the most powerful tool you have for change.

When you access the goodwill you have inside you, you will immediately begin to feel happier, more in control, more open to changes and better able to make decisions. Those around you will react to you in a more positive way too. Goodwill can cut through red tape, hostility, shyness, doubt and fear.

If you are in a difficult situation, facing a decision, under pressure or overburdened, then you may be feeling tired, angry, frustrated, resentful, sad or hurt. Without pushing any of these feelings away, look deep inside yourself and find the goodwill you always have there. If it is buried a long way down, tucked away in a corner or shut inside a box, then let it out, dust it off and gently bring it up to the surface, so that you can feel it more strongly than any other feeling. If you are struggling to find it, be patient and know that it is there. Often what stands between you and your goodwill is your defensiveness. What if it was OK to be wrong, to make mistakes and to be who you are under these circumstances? When you let go of having to be right, even though you might be, then it's easy to find your goodwill.

Think of times when getting in touch with your goodwill really worked for you and remember what it felt like. Your goodwill is your ally. No matter how angry, hurt or frustrated you feel, your goodwill is there, waiting to help you. Do not confuse goodwill with weakness, letting yourself be pushed around or giving in inappropriately. Goodwill isn't about saying yes to everything – you can say no with goodwill. True goodwill includes self-respect and setting clear boundaries.

Use your goodwill, let it act for you and take charge of the situation and watch as things turn around. Confronting angrily, attacking and trying to control others will only result in battles, sulking and non-cooperation. But goodwill is like a magnet. It will attract the goodwill of others. When you bring goodwill to a situation it is like inviting the sun to come out. Everything will become easier, simpler and more pleasant.

To find goodwill is not to back down, give in or lose face. It is simply to be willing to find the best possible outcome for yourself and others in any situation. Let goodwill be your most powerful friend.

Connecting Through Stillness

When you open this book here, know that it is time to slow down and be with yourself.

If you already practise the arts of meditation and yoga, you should check that you are bringing the highest level of calm and focus to the process so that you can be sure to find yourself within it. Go even more slowly, concentrate on your sense of existing rather than on getting it right or doing it better. The whole point is to strip yourself of your ego to experience your true self.

For all of us, the key to stillness is to spend time focusing on your breathing, even if you can only keep your attention on a few breaths at a time. Make sure that you breathe in and out through your nostrils and that your ribcage expands on the in-breath and contracts with the out-breath. Breathe slowly, as if you are feeding a thread in and out and you don't want to go so fast that you tangle it. It sounds simple, but you'd be amazed how many people have muddled up the basic breathing pattern of life.

Right now you need to connect with yourself. You are keeping busy because you are scared of being with the feelings that you are avoiding. Know that the pain and energy around feelings comes from resisting them, rather than feeling them. When you feel them you will know relief and they will be released. When it feels as though your feelings overwhelm you, the challenge is to trust that they won't.

If you are very resistant to stillness at the moment, find safe ways to move towards increasing the levels of calm in your body and mind. Turn the phone and TV off, dim the lights and put on some calming music. Have a candlelit bath and let your mind drift rather than work. Go for a long walk or do something physically demanding like cleaning, painting or gardening. Each time you notice yourself thinking, just let the thought go. Don't use this time to do any mental tasks. The more you practise this, the more likely it is that you will experience moments of connecting with universal energy and the sense that we are all part of a single cosmic identity.

This place is where the safety and the wisdom lies. This is where we have our best insights, our guidance from above and our sense that we are pure and good whatever experiences life hands us. The more you tap into it, the better you will know how to deal with what is present in your life right now and the richer you will be. Begin at a level which feels comfortable for you, and work at developing connection through stillness, for therein lies true peace and contentment.

Conflict

W hen you open this book here, it is to remind you of the value and importance of conflict in your life.

To be in conflict is to be in a fight, struggle or clash with someone else or within yourself. Conflict with others is a necessary, normal and healthy part of life. What matters is to handle this in a way that leaves you and others with self-respect.

Look at your own conflict patterns. Do you pick fights often? Do you refuse to alter your view or respect that of the other person, no matter what? Do you think you're always in the right? Or are you afraid of conflict, keeping your mouth shut to avoid rows and seething silently instead? Whichever approach you take, it is time to put conflict into perspective in your life and to learn to handle it with confidence and skill.

Conflict should never, ever involve physical violence. It should never involve verbal abuse, put-downs or unkindness to yourself or others. To handle conflict well you need to respect your own opinion as well as the other person's right to have theirs. Conflict is appropriate when it involves standing up for yourself and your beliefs or for the rights of someone who is genuinely helpless. It is a way of defining yourself and your position in the world.

The goal is to come away from conflict with your head held high and your self-esteem strong. That means treating those you are in conflict with decently and with respect, even when you are angry. It means holding your ground while being willing to shift positions if there is a good reason to. It means being willing to live with your differences while knowing what your bottom line is, as well as knowing when to protect yourself by walking away.

If you are in conflict right now, stand back from the situation for a moment and decide what is needed. If the conflict hasn't been acknowledged, now is the time to admit what is bubbling under the surface. Is it time to reconsider, or to hold firm to your beliefs? Be willing to work towards ending the conflict with the best possible outcome for everyone involved. If the conflict you are in at the moment is inside yourself, then acknowledge it and treat yourself with kindness and compassion. Don't judge or punish yourself, and allow yourself time to come to the best possible decision or conclusion.

Use conflict as a way to acknowledge the need to move forward, to grow and to learn more about who you are and what really matters to you.

Goals

When you open this book here, it is to encourage you to focus on what it is that you want in relation to your life or current circumstances. You have to know where you want to go if you are to get there.

A goal is the purpose, outcome or resting place which our endeavours are directed towards. Stop and review what you are trying to accomplish. It is surprising how often we are involved in tasks without any real sense of what we want. What do you want?

Get a pen and paper and write a list of what you want, then keep reviewing this for a couple of days and update it as your ideas and opinions become clearer to you. This is a useful exercise to get more honest about what your goals are. You may start with what seems like an ambitious goal but, as you get used to it, it may well start to seem achievable and safe. Over time, you will get braver and more demanding and end up with exciting, new and challenging goals that originally you didn't even let yourself aspire to. Or you may be forced to admit how unrealistic your goals have been and get more realistic.

Know that your goals are personal to you and that it is unimportant what others think of them. You need to find your purpose, your targets and what motivates you, as opposed to what you think your goals *should* be. You are unique, so your goals may well be very unique too. Or they may be totally predictable and conventional. It doesn't matter as long as you're clear about what you want.

For goals to work they need to be very specific. It's no good just saying that you want to be rich, that you want a new job, a relationship, or a family. You need to know how rich and by when, what kind of relationship, what sort of job. The universe delivers our dreams to us when we are clear about what they are and make constructive and decisive moves to bring them into being. Break your dream up into tangible, achievable elements. Few people go from nothing to suddenly reaching their ultimate goal – there are always steps along the way. Even lottery winners have to buy the ticket and choose their numbers. Work out what your steps are and how you can accomplish them. And be willing to put in the effort it may take to achieve them.

Create the image of the future in the present and then let reality catch up. Talk about when you accomplish your goals, not if. See yourself creating the results that you desire and believe in yourself. Commit your goal to paper with a date for when it will be accomplished and sign it. Now go for it. It can be done.

Getting Hooked

When you open this book here, it is because you are getting hooked on something or someone and it is not doing you any good.

The time has come to unhook yourself and let go. Being hooked is just what it sounds like — uncomfortable and frustrating. It is also painful and leaves you feeling helpless. Imagine a fish, caught on the angler's hook, struggling and fighting to free itself. You are hooked too, but there is a difference. For unlike the fish, you let yourself become hooked in the first place, and you can choose to free yourself.

Being hooked brings out stubbornness and obsession in us all. It happens to everyone now and then, sometimes for a short while, and sometimes for years. When you are hooked you go into denial. You refuse to see the damage you are doing to yourself or others. You refuse to see how much your being hooked controls your life and shuts out other possibilities. You may even tell yourself that you are happy about being hooked. But whatever it is you are hooked on, whether it is a person you long to be close to, a sport you devote every free hour to, a habit, or a set of rules, principles or beliefs, know that to follow anything to an extreme level is always a way of avoiding something else which you need to pay attention to. Check out what or who you are hooked by right now. Is it really so important? What would happen if you stepped back or created calm in this situation?

Frequently, we unhook from one thing only to get hooked by another. We can't bear to be free. Think about what being hooked helps you to avoid. What would you focus on if you weren't so busy being passionate about something or someone else? Getting hooked is a way of avoiding issues and feelings in your life, but all it does is let the issues and feelings build up which sooner or later need to be faced.

Be brave, unhook yourself and take charge of your life. You will have to go through the discomfort of unhooking and dealing with what you have been avoiding, but what will follow will more than make up for it. You'll feel relief, you'll be able to really know yourself and get your life back into balance, and that will open you up to real joy. Take the first step forward, it is enough for today.

Moving On

When you open this book here, it reminds you of the importance of moving on and letting go of all that is finished with, all that is no longer useful or anything damaging or unhelpful in your life. What is it you need to move on from? Whether it is a job, a romantic relationship, a home, a friend, a place, a habit, an addiction or a routine, you are staying attached to it when it would be better for you to move on. It's time for something new, now.

It is fear which keeps us attached to something or someone we have outgrown, or to something which is actually doing us harm and lowering our self-esteem. We become afraid of loss, of change, of never finding anything better to fill the gap left in our lives, or of criticism from others who don't want us to move on.

Dealing with the fear is the key to moving on successfully. Be honest with yourself about your fears. What do you imagine would happen if you moved on? What is it you don't want to look at? Know that it is far worse to stay attached to something through fear than to face the consequences of letting it go. To move on, you have to be willing to take a leap of faith and to trust your own judgement, especially if others are discouraging you. Recognise that you have the power to make decisions about your life and to move on when you want to. You will also have to deal with any old and unfinished business which is holding you back.

Often we refuse to move on until the pain of staying with what we have grows larger than our fear of letting it go. If this is the place that you have reached, know that the time is right to free yourself to make whatever changes and choices you need in your life. And then, although you may feel some sadness for what you have left behind, you will also feel enormous relief, optimism and a sense of freedom and power.

Moving on is natural and appropriate at many stages in life. And to know when to move on is vital if you are to take the next step along the path to happiness and fulfilment. Trust that you do know when it is time to move on and that you can do it successfully. You can.

Passivity

When you open this book here, the issue to address is that of passivity. This can take many forms, but in the end it all boils down to one fundamental issue – that of being submissive. Allowing events or other people to influence you without engaging in appropriate levels of participation or resistance.

When you are passive you play the victim. Of course, when you act as the victim you may not recognise it as such. Instead, you will see yourself as hard done by or the subject of circumstances or events outside your control. Know that this interpretation is all part of your passivity, it is exactly how you maintain your victim position.

What do you need to look at in a new light right now? What do you need to take responsibility for? What do you need to control and direct that you currently think you are powerless around or are playing dumb about? At the end of the day, only you will be responsible for who you are and how your life turned out. There really is no satisfaction in looking back on a life that didn't live up to your expectations and then justifying the way it went. All the justifications in the world won't bring back the life that you could have had but let pass you by. So don't let it happen.

It may be that you feel thwarted and frustrated by the passivity of others around you at the moment. Know that there is absolutely nothing that you can do about this, other than to clarify your feelings and then to get active yourself. Leave other people out of it and focus on yourself. Imagine everyone else was always going to stay the same and then start deciding on what path you will take, given this.

You are only powerless when you give away or reject your power, looking to others or fate to create your destiny. Know that the universal forces will only work with you when you get working yourself. If you sit around waiting, you will wait for ever. Make it happen for yourself.

Create your own destiny, cast aside passivity and enjoy being in the driver's seat. The more you do it, the more you'll love it.

Visualisation

When you open this book here, it is to remind you of the power and value of visualisation in bringing about the changes that you want in your life.

To visualise is to see in your mind. When you visualise, you create mental pictures of your life, and because universal law is such that we create our own world and draw to us the things in it, visualisation carries tremendous power. Your life will be what you expect it to be and what you believe it will be. So when you begin to change your expectations and beliefs you will see the results appearing all around you. Never underestimate the power of this process. Understand that what you have now is what you believe you deserve and can have. It is what you have already visualised. If you want more of this, or if you want something different, whether it is in the area of love, friendship, children, work, understanding, wealth, skills or anything else, then use the power of visualisation.

We all have imagination, no matter how seldom we use it. Bring yours out and let it grow, feeding it with ideas and encouraging it with time and space. Lie or sit down for ten minutes and picture what it is that you want in beautiful, colourful detail. Tell yourself this is your right and that it will come to you soon. If you struggle with creating pictures in your mind make yourself a picture scrap-book of the right images to make the ideas more real for you. Appreciate the skill you have already shown in drawing the good things you already have to you and know that you can extend this skill to any area of your life.

If it is a relationship or job you want, or if you wish to see something resolved positively, then concentrate on creating a picture of yourself in this scenario. Be specific about your part in the outcome, about how you will feel and what you will do. See them fitting in with what you want and benefiting too, but don't try too hard to control others as you are only free to control yourself.

Let the power of visualisation be a valuable tool in creating the life that you want. Know that what you see inside will be what you see outside and that it is all up to you.

Healing

When you open this book here, be glad because the message is a wonderful one. It is time to let healing take place within yourself and your life, and to open yourself to the possibility of having vibrant good health and positive energy in this area of your life.

To heal is to cure or to restore to health. What is it that needs healing right now? Is there a relationship or a situation which is painful or difficult for you? Is your health low, have you injured yourself or are you unwell? Or is it your confidence, your ability to love, your trust or your belief in yourself which needs healing?

Whatever it is, know that healing is absolutely possible and you have everything you need to bring it about. Let others play their part in your healing where it is appropriate, but know that only you know what is really needed. When you believe that you can heal yourself, you will find that you are able to do this.

The first step in healing is acceptance. Allow yourself to accept completely whatever it is you feel and whatever your situation is. Don't fight it, criticise yourself or struggle to change anything right now. Healing is best done gently. Allow a sense of peace into your heart. Let the love and understanding in your soul shine through and illuminate the situation. Ask yourself what benefits the painful feelings, difficulties, ill health or broken relationships have brought you. Know that there is always a benefit and that you are stronger and wiser for going through these difficulties.

Sometimes during healing there is a 'healing crisis' when the problem appears to be worse than it was at the beginning. We get sicker, the pain gets worse, the problem seems harder to solve. Don't be afraid if this happens to you – it is a good thing because it means that healing is taking place. It is simply what is underneath coming to the surface in order to be cleared. Just accept what is happening and trust that it will pass. Give yourself time to heal, nurture yourself and trust your own wisdom to know what it is that you need.

Let go of any resistance you have, let go of the fear of going through the healing process. Healing is taking place, fighting it will only delay it. All you have to do is allow it to continue in your life.

Feelings Follow Behaviour

When you open this book here, it is to remind you of one of life's most important guiding principles: that our feelings follow our behaviour. When we act in a certain way, our bodies send messages to our brains about how we are feeling, not the other way around. Thus if we are lethargic and adopt a depressed posture we will feel depressed. When we are light on our feet and moving freely, however, we will feel free and optimistic.

How are you feeling? If you are content and satisfied, then know that the way you are behaving is working and stick with it. But if you are down about things, know that you are creating your own reality and that you do have a choice. If you took a different approach to what you do, you would start to feel different and in turn this would have a positive knock-on effect on other areas of your behaviour and your life.

Maybe you're doing what you've always done. Humans are creatures of habit and when things don't go the way we want them to we often get caught up in doing more of the same thing in an effort to get the result we want. The trouble is that then we end up feeling the same, only more so. What could you do differently right now? How could you act differently? As soon as you change your physiology, by moving in a new way, and change your actions and the way you look at things, you will feel different.

If you want to feel happier, act happy. If you want to feel confident, act confidently. If you want to feel motivated, behave in a way that someone who is motivated would behave.

We can wait for ever to feel in the mood to do something and that mood may never come, but if we just get up and get started the feelings will follow the behaviour and the mood for doing what we are doing will come upon us as if by magic.

The fact that feelings follow behaviour is an incredible and useful reality. It means that the power lies in positive action and behaviour, no matter how scared or resistant we may feel about that action. Use it to your advantage and you can find a resolution to every issue.

Blessing

When you open this book here, you can afford to be excited and optimistic. Whatever issue you are focused upon is blessed at this moment in time.

This means that it should provide you with great happiness or a sense of satisfaction. If things are good, rejoice and relax and let yourself enjoy this positive time. If things are difficult or you are struggling with a painful issue, know that when we receive a Blessing, the protection and influence of the divine has been invoked to watch over us and guide us through these experiences. We may each have a different interpretation of this divinity, be it God, your higher power or the positive universal energies, but whatever the form of your divinity, the result will be the same. And this will hold true regardless of what you believe in.

The Blessing reassures you that right now you are on the right path. You have found your way and things should go according to your wishes, hopes and dreams. If they take an unexpected turn, go with it, stay active and responsible to yourself and others, but know that you are guided and that all will be well.

When something is blessed it is worthy of reverence and respect.

Remember to let things be what they are, rather than trying to force them to be something else. This is a time to feed your soul and fill your life with the things that positively enrich you.

Now is a good time to make the most of the divine energy around you. Take action which you know to be in your best interest, be brave, be determined, be optimistic. Hug your Blessing to yourself and move forward in a constructive and satisfying way. Trust in the divine and carry with you the knowledge that what you are undertaking is Blessed.

Responsibility

When you open this book here, it is time to recognise the importance of responsibility in your life.

Often responsibility is seen as boring and dull. It is associated with restriction, lack of choice, burdens and financial ties. Do you see responsibility in this way and avoid it in particular areas of your life? Well, now is the time to think again and to understand the true nature of responsibility and the value it can bring you.

When you avoid responsibility, you blame others and see yourself as helpless. To take responsibility is to learn how to respond appropriately to any situation you are faced with, and to recognise that whatever you do in life is your own choice. It means to act with care, thoughtfulness and respect, to be trustworthy and to be willing to account for your actions. To be responsible is to be adult in the truest, most satisfying way.

To be responsible, you must be willing to follow through on the choices you have made and to fulfil the obligations you have undertaken to others, or to renegotiate your responsibilities as and when this is appropriate.

And yet there are times when responsibility is used as an excuse for avoiding action or facing the truth. Sometimes we can convince ourselves that we are responsible for another person, but it is only ever appropriate to be responsible for a child. Adults are responsible for themselves and although some responsibilities can be shared between you, that does not mean you are responsible for the life or the choices of another adult.

The greatest responsibility you will ever have is to yourself. When you prioritise this, then your responsibilities to others will flow easily and be a pleasure rather than a burden. You are responsible for treating yourself well, for listening to your own feelings and for making sure that your behaviour is always honest, compassionate and trustworthy towards yourself and others. To be responsible is to free yourself from the restrictions others try to place upon you and to choose for yourself the path you will take. Start today.

Releasing

When you open this book here, it is time to release beliefs and behaviours which are damaging you or holding you back. These are usually beliefs and ways of behaving which you learnt earlier in life and which served a useful purpose then but are no longer necessary or useful to you now.

Do you avoid speaking up for yourself and asking for what you want? Do you feel you only have value if you are looking after others or working hard? Or do you charge through life making demands and being harsh on yourself and others? How is what you do or what you believe creating what is going on right now or preventing you from moving forward?

These ways of thinking and behaving, and others which are unhelpful, developed in childhood as ways of coping with difficulties which were beyond your control. Recognise this and don't be hard on yourself. Appreciate that you tried your best and did what worked at the time.

Now is the time to set about releasing these behaviours and the beliefs behind them and replacing them with behaviours and beliefs which you like and which you can feel proud of.

When you can change your beliefs, your behaviour will follow and vice versa. Get clear about the beliefs and behaviours that you don't like and that don't work for you. Now is the time to release them. Know that it takes time and effort to really let go of behaviours and beliefs which you have relied on for many years.

The ability to change begins with releasing. Let go of what no longer serves you and create the life that you want.

In order to release behaviours that are not of benefit, you need to replace them with new behaviours. You must actually do something different. With beliefs, however, you will need to concentrate on releasing the old beliefs, as it is only after you do this that you can effectively replace them with new ones. Include the belief that you want to release in a sentence which starts with 'I release the need to believe . . .' and repeat it as often as possible. After this, you can create a sentence which includes the new belief to take its place.

Keep repeating your releasing statements and practising your new behaviours and feel the relief and clarity of knowing that you can change.

Keep on releasing more and more and discover how liberating it can be in your life. It's time to let it go.

Challenge

When you open this book here, it is because you are facing an important challenge. Life is presenting you with the opportunity to deal with someone or something which will demand that you stretch yourself beyond what is easy, what you know or what is comfortable for you.

This is a real gift. A fabulous opportunity to show yourself and others that there is more to you and that you can extend yourself in positive and constructive ways.

It is time for you to question the established order. To review how you do things and why. To get clear about what your position and opinion is under these circumstances, and to decide how you will go forward from here.

Know that you are up to this challenge or it would not be presenting itself to you in this way, right now. But this does not mean that the outcome is a foregone conclusion. At this moment the outcome is undefined. It depends upon you and how you rise to the challenge.

Sometimes we need to go head first into the fray with all our strength and determination, while other instances demand much more subtle and sensitive handling. Take time to work out which this is.

Know that whatever you are dealing with, it is appropriate for you to be stretched by this. You should find it challenging and you will need your ingenuity, but if you give it your best you will not be the same person after this as you were before. You will have a richer, deeper understanding of yourself and the world and you will go forward with greater confidence and trust, knowing that you can handle life and what it demands of you. Remember that diamonds are created under extreme pressure.

The real challenge is to work out what this experience is mirroring for you from your past, and particularly your childhood, that you still need to deal with and resolve. Every challenge is a healing crisis. An opportunity to address those long-buried patterns and pains of our earlier lives that get repeated over and over, whether from the same side of the coin or from the opposite side, until we make the connection and free ourselves from their grip. But we can only do this by facing the truth.

It may be demanding, but know that you are ready or this challenge would not have appeared. You can do it. So start now.

Unmet Needs

When you open this book here, it is to draw your attention to your unmet needs. What is it that you require right now that you are not getting in your life? What is it that keeps getting put off or neglected? That you don't get around to dealing with or attending to? This is a warning that the issue to hand is a direct result of your needs not being met or your attempt to distract yourself and others from the fact that you actually have needs. So if you want life to work out as you'd like it to, you must address your unmet needs now.

This doesn't mean that you need to be totally self-centred and irresponsible, although prioritising yourself may make you feel this way sometimes.

Know that we all have needs, all the time. It is part of being human. We need food and shelter, warmth, rest, physical safety and human contact. We need relationships with others and a good relationship with ourselves. We need a sense of purpose and a sense of belonging in our lives. We need life to have predictable elements and stability as well as stimulation, excitement and adventure. We need to be appreciated and to have a sense that in some way we contribute to our world.

What is it that you need at the moment? Know that when you are critical and judgemental you will have an unmet need lurking around somewhere.

Don't worry if you're not sure what your needs are at the moment. Start by simply acknowledging what this is telling you: that you have unmet needs. Next consider what it is that you would want if you could have anything. If the idea seems achievable then work out how to get it. If it seems totally out of reach, then break it up into smaller elements or moderate it. A trip around the world could become a five-year long-term plan or a city break next month. The need for a month on a desert island may actually mean that you simply need a few hours extra sleep, a hug and some sunshine. An hour-long cry may actually be finished in ten minutes if you would only let yourself have it.

Be sure to check whether you are spending too much time trying to meet someone else's needs in the hope that your needs will be met after theirs. Be warned that it doesn't work like this. You have to put your focus on yourself and make yourself the priority. If you keep putting your needs off, the consequences of living like this will be enormous. It leads to bitterness, resentment, anger and ill health. Then you'll have a whole different set of needs to attend to!

Now is the time to look after yourself properly by getting your needs met.

Go on, give yourself what you need and reap the benefits.

Grandiosity

When you open this book here, know that the issue you need to face right now is grandiosity, which means trying to appear great, clever or powerful.

Look carefully at the ways in which you are doing this. It may be in one area of your life or several. It may take the form of trying to impress one person or many. It may be blatant, such as boasting or making over-generous promises, or it may be well concealed behind a quietly virtuous appearance. You may feel that you are justified in blowing your own trumpet, but be aware of the difference between pride and pleasure in who you are and your achievements, and grandiosity, which is unrealistic, arrogant or pompous and intended only to impress.

It may be painful to recognise the ways in which you are grandiose, but it is vital to catch it and to stop acting in this way. Grandiosity is always a cover-up for insecurity and convinces no one except those who are like-minded. It attracts only dislike, boredom, ridicule or pity from others. When you put yourself on a pedestal there is only one way to fall, for the universe will be determined to teach you the lesson of humility.

The key to letting go of grandiosity is to admit to your fearfulness and insecurity. The minute you do this you will realise that these feelings aren't so terrible after all and that there is no need to hide them in the way that you attempt to. If you are honest with others about who you are and what you feel, they will warm to you, respect your honesty and want to be closer to you. Be authentic and you will always attract a positive response from others.

Instead of trying to impress others, impress yourself with your courage in facing your fears. Recognise your real talents and abilities and that the pleasure you can gain from them is your own satisfaction. Let the energy you put into trying to create a grand image to impress others go into nurturing and caring for yourself.

The more genuine, honest and open you are, the greater your confidence will be and the more pleasure you will gain from sharing with others. Instead of trying to impress people, be your real self and you'll find it's much more fun.

Acceptance

When you open this book here, be at peace and know that all you have to do is to accept what is happening in your life right now, and this in itself will create change. To accept means to live with and tolerate whatever is going on, rather than running away from it or struggling to change it.

This may feel very challenging because sometimes the hardest thing of all is to do nothing. If things in your life are difficult, uncomfortable or painful then it can be much easier to put all your energy into figuring out ways to change either events, yourself or other people. And sometimes that's the answer. But not this time. What's needed now is less action, less struggle and more peaceful, calm acceptance that, however unlikely it seems at the moment, everything is happening just the way it needs to for your greater good.

Stop fighting with life, take a deep breath, relax all your muscles and let what is be enough. Instead of putting your energy into the outside world to create change, turn it inwards and use it for yourself. Be gentle and loving with yourself while you are learning to accept whatever needs accepting. Don't make it another chore.

Recognise the importance of handing the issue over to a higher power and trusting that it will sort everything out and create the best possible outcome. Acceptance involves discovering that you don't know how things will turn out and that that's OK. It isn't all up to you. Whether you have deep spiritual beliefs or not, know that there are powerful energies working around you right now which will protect you and bring about what you most need – although that isn't always the same as what you may think you need.

Discover the joy and relief in acceptance. Let go of trying to control everything and let it all be. Sleep, go for a walk, write out your feelings, laugh with friends, do whatever feels good. Don't neglect your responsibilities, but trust that acceptance is the way forward for you, that at the moment doing less will create more and that when you stand back events will shift in ways which will amaze you.

You Get Back What You Put In

W hen you open this book here, it is time to think about the contribution you are making, or have been making, to what is going on around you.

In life you get back what you put in, so if things are going well, know that you are being rewarded for your efforts. This has not come to you out of the blue, you have earned it for yourself. Now all you have to do is to reap the benefits while recognising that this is how life works. Use this success to inspire you to create the future you want through your actions now.

Know that the universe works on an 'energy in, energy out' basis. When your efforts are rewarded, it is because of the relationship between the energy that you put into something and what comes back to you in your life. It means that you are putting in constructive effort and a positive belief in the outcome. When your efforts are not rewarded it means that some part of you does not believe that you can get what you want or that you deserve it. It can also mean that your efforts are not those which are necessary or useful, given the circumstances. What could you do differently? Are you putting yourself out into the world or are you hiding where it feels safe? The energy you put into sharpening pencils or organising yourself is valid as a starting point, but you will not get what you want by avoiding reaching out. Energy put into diversions and distractions will not bring you inner peace — it will simply bring you diversions and distractions.

Check where your energy is going. If you are particularly passive and inactive right now, know that you are using your energy to create this in your life. Your reward is more of the same. If you want something to change, then put in what it is that you want to get back.

Sometimes what you need is to be persistent. When we stick at something that we really believe in, we see a result that is worthy of our continued efforts. If you want it badly enough, then be determined and keep at it until you get the result you are looking for.

Remember that thoughts dominate and create your reality, so this is where the greatest power to get back what you put in lies. But we live in a physical, material world, so thoughts need to be backed up by action. The power is all yours, so use it.

Freedom

When you open this book here, it is to let you know that you are being constrained and controlled by outside influences and that it is time to break free. This is not to suggest that reckless, indiscriminate action is the answer, but rather that you need to consider how much of your current situation and how many of your decisions are being controlled by your reliance on something or someone else.

Are you free to make your own decisions and to come to your own conclusions, or are you hemmed in by the requirements of those around you? Do you know where you stand on key issues, what you would like to do and what you really want? So often we think that we are free, but create our own limits by being unable to move in a direction that is not approved by those around us. Or we imprison ourselves with our own views and judgements about who we should be and how we should live, without ever really freeing ourselves to make our own decisions and rules about this.

How many rules do you make up for yourself about the way you should live your life, how you should behave? Do you recognise these simply as rules that you have made up or do you believe them to be established reality? What would happen if you broke the rules? Who would you be then? How would it feel?

You opened the book here because it is time for you to begin freeing yourself, on both the big and the little issues. While respecting others, it is time for you to truly establish your own opinions and choices. To come clean about what you really want and to stop trying to get what you want through coercing or manipulating others. To stop pretending that you want what you think you can have, or what you think that others want you to want or have. To stop guessing who you are meant to be and to be free to be yourself.

Freedom presents the ultimate challenge because when you allow yourself to be free you allow others to be free too. Then you have to live with and react to who they really are, rather than staying caught up in trying to change them.

Let freedom be your guide and enjoy the liberation it brings to your life.

Keep It Simple

When you open this book here it is because there is the pressing need to keep things simple in your life right now. This is the approach to take if you wish to solve your problems or accomplish your goals.

We live in a complicated world. Never before have we had so many choices or options available to us. But often this only serves to involve us in unnecessary confusion or complexity. Is your life out of balance right now? Do you want to achieve something but you don't know where to start? Are you struggling with the decisions that you have to make? Do you feel you have too many balls in the air for you to keep juggling them all successfully? Or perhaps things are going really well at the moment and you want to know how to keep them like that.

The answer to all of your questions is to focus on keeping things simple. Start with what is most immediate rather than planning so far ahead that you trip yourself up or waste energy on something that may never happen. How could you simplify things today? What could you do differently? What would you have to stop doing?

Without being irresponsible, put the focus on yourself and your needs because it is when we try to control or please others that things stop being simple and stop working for us. Sometimes the hardest thing about keeping things simple is that we have to admit our limitations and let other people down. We have to be willing to take the consequences of letting go of the complex web that we have woven. But if we learn from how we have over-stretched or over committed ourselves, doing this will be for the best. And when we accept that we are powerless over how others feel or act then we can put all the energy we use trying to keep them sweet into making our own lives work instead.

Keeping it simple means being honest with yourself and others. It means letting go of the many distractions that making life complicated provides for you. It means admitting when you already know what the answer to your question is and getting on with it. And when you don't know the answer it means seeking the simplest and most straightforward solution that works for you, instead of going around in circles to avoid having to act.

When we put one foot in front of the other and do what needs to be done and say what needs to be said, then we begin to feel the benefits of this simplicity. Now is the time to find your own truth and your own priorities. Be brave and although life may be bumpy in the short run, you will soon reap the benefits and see that the solution always lies in keeping it simple.

Parenting

When you open this book here, it is because you need to address parenting issues. These issues may be about your children, other children in your life, the child within you or another adult that you are treating like a child.

Few of us were parented in such a healthy and balanced manner that we do not develop with some part of us from our childhood days cut off and buried within. And this part is still longing for whatever was denied to us back then. As we mature, we find that we need to go back and love and parent this inner child in order to be happy and successful in our day-to-day lives. Parenting children and parenting your inner child require exactly the same skills and are equally important. Learning to do either will help you to transfer the skills from one task to the other. It is vital to remember that both aspects of parenting exist. Otherwise you will end up projecting your inner needs or aspirations on to the children in your life, living through them unfairly while failing to meet your own needs. Or you may hold yourself back from having children because you cannot even parent yourself. Make sure too that you aren't acting like a parent to another adult

– especially your own parents or your partner – because this is inappropriate.

Are you struggling to make a decision right now? Are you concerned with what is the best action to take or what to do next? When we are parents, we are guardians to another who relies on us to keep them safe and teach them the best way to be in the world. Other times it's ourselves we have to teach this to. While our words carry heavy influence, you need to remember that what dominates is always what we do rather than what we say. Be kind to yourself and any child in your care, but remember that kindness involves boundaries and responsibility. It isn't about saying yes all the time but about showing that we have choices and that all choices have consequences, whether good or bad.

Are you sufficiently available in your parenting, both physically and emotionally? Are you sufficiently caring and gentle? To develop, we all need nurturing and support and when we grow up we need to learn to parent ourselves in this way. To be tolerant and accepting of the wealth of emotions the child or inner child experiences, and to teach them how to experience these emotions in a safe and responsible manner.

Parenting asks you to reclaim your power as a positive nurturing and supportive force. Deal with whatever is required now and remember to get support for yourself while you do. Good parents don't exist in a vacuum.

Recharge

When you open this book here, take heart. Whatever is not working or happening in your life at the moment will shift once you recharge yourself.

Right now your energy is low and you are running your life on an empty tank. When we do this things simply stop working around us and life seems difficult and exhausting. Suddenly you can't find parking spaces or your car breaks down, you get irritable with other people, you produce work you're not happy with or you develop health problems.

Does this sound familiar? Are you driving yourself on at full pace, ignoring or dismissing the warning signs? If so, stop right now. Trust that all will be well and that everything will get simpler and easier once you do the one thing you're not doing – which is to look after yourself properly.

Recharging means resting and recuperating. It means taking time out from life's usual hectic pace and putting yourself and your needs first. Spend a day in bed with a good novel, eat nourishing food, take gentle exercise, write a journal.

And while you do these things look honestly at where your

energy is going. Are you doing too much for others? Trying to please or win approval? Being a perfectionist? Or propping someone up emotionally? Well, now's the time to start doing things differently, so that in future you won't struggle along on a flat battery.

Start to delegate jobs to others, at home or at work. Be less of a perfectionist, walk past jobs that can wait, accept that someone else's way of doing things will do just as well as yours and let people learn to solve their own problems. Most important of all, keep looking after yourself. That means putting yourself first and making sure that your needs for rest, good food, space, companionship, fun and relaxation are met. Don't worry about being selfish, you'll give more easily and generously to others when you care properly for yourself.

If you ignore this warning, eventually circumstances will conspire to force you to recharge. So take control instead, take the time to recharge and give yourself the gift of compassion and love.

Choice

When you open this book here, it is a reminder that you always have a choice about what you do and how you do it.

Sometimes it can seem as though you have no choice, but that is simply because you are afraid to look at what the choices really are. The alternatives may seem scary, unpredictable or too hard, so you reject them by telling yourself that they aren't really available. Know that, whatever your situation right now, there are always alternatives available. Be brave and honest about facing them and understanding that the outcome of your situation will be of your own choosing.

With choice comes responsibility and freedom. You have the responsibility to choose carefully and well, with respect and consideration for those involved, including yourself. And you have the freedom to choose how to respond, which turns you from a helpless victim into someone who has power and a say in any situation.

Choice involves decision-making, weighing up the pros and cons, playing safe or taking risks and considering all the possible consequences. As children we had fewer choices to make and we learned how to make choices only on a small scale. As adults we hold the power over our own lives and destinies and all the choices are ours. But some of us continue to behave like children, believing that we have few choices and that others control us. If this is you, it is time to stop. Know that every situation in your life is of your own choosing and that you make the choices, whether you are aware of them or not.

Begin to make choices consciously, with pleasure and a sense of purpose and self-respect. Be proud of your choices and value the possibilities they bring into your life.

You may feel that you are at the mercy of your reactions when something makes you sad or angry, and you feel frustrated that people or events are not as you would choose them to be. But though you have no choice about the way you feel, you always have a choice about how you react. You have a choice about how you act and behave in each moment of feeling. You can speak up and own your reality when you don't like something, even if you can't change it. You have the choice to be you.

Avoiding Feelings

When you open this book here, it is because you have painful feelings which you are trying to avoid. You are putting enormous energy into avoiding them, but it isn't working and all you are doing is giving yourself a hard time.

Painful feelings like anger, sadness, hurt, grief, jealousy, or a mixture of several of these, can be so frightening and feel so unacceptable that it seems easier to stuff them down inside, so far out of sight that most of the time you don't even remember that they're there. Or you can be so cut off from the feelings that you are avoiding that you couldn't label them even if you let yourself have them. Life can feel like a dark, black, empty place or a whirl of activity and distraction with little feeling in it at all.

The trouble is that you have to work very hard to keep your feelings shut off, to keep pretending they're not there. Huge dollops of your energy are spent on keeping the feelings locked in and developing behaviours which are designed to cover up painful feelings and distract you from them.

Often these behaviours are addictive and compulsive. You feel driven to do them even when you may not really want to, even when you know that they are harming you and don't really work or make you feel better.

As well as recognised addictions such as drinking, smoking, drug-taking, spending, over-eating and under-eating, there are dozens of other less obvious addictions which many of us use to keep our painful feelings buried. Do you consistently work long hours? Are you always cleaning and tidying? Do you take prescription drugs such as anti-depressants or tranquillisers, both of which are simply feeling suppressants? Or do you keep yourself relentlessly busy, always rushing from one thing to the next, never finished with your list of things to do? If you recognise yourself, then know that whatever it is you are doing is a cover-up and it's time to stop and free yourself. Whatever the surface issue is right now, avoiding your feelings is the real issue.

Stopping addictive behaviour isn't easy, but it's always possible and it's a choice you have to make. To stop and stay stopped, rather than just replacing one addiction with another, you will need to get help. You must find the courage to face the feelings you are avoiding and trace them back to your original childhood pain. As children we learned to cope with unbearable pain by pushing it inside. As adults we can learn to cope with what we have been avoiding.

Painful feelings are released when they are faced. Remember that the only way out is through.

Thought

When you open this book here, it is to let you know that you have within you a source of enormous power for change and creativity which you can tap into at any time, and which you can use to address whatever it is that you are dealing with right now.

The thoughts in your mind are as real as any kind of signal and message service which we have in the material world – and far more powerful. Thoughts are living, tangible beings which create the reality of your life. The thought comes first and then life pulls itself into line with it.

Your thoughts are private but the results are not. They are everywhere in your life, your relationships, your behaviour patterns and your circumstances. Look around and what you will see are your thoughts reflected back to you from your circumstances and surroundings.

Because of this, it is important to respect the power of thought and to choose your thoughts with care. Your thoughts are based on your beliefs, so when you have thoughts which are destructive, unkind or self-denying, then look for the belief behind them and change it for a more positive, constructive one. This takes effort, but it can be done and the results will be worth it.

If you believe that you don't deserve success, happiness and good things in life, then you will use your thoughts to make sure that your belief comes true. You'll tell yourself that you're not clever enough, good enough or loveable enough to have what you want. And then you won't get whatever it is, or you won't be able to keep it. If you have good in your life, know that it is because of the way you have been thinking in this area – and that you can use this ability for other issues too.

Use your thoughts to change your beliefs. Tell yourself that you are clever, good and loveable enough to have exactly what you want. Play these thoughts over and over to yourself. Create, in your mind, the thoughts you would like others to have about you and the things you would like to bring into your life. Send out goodwill and healing energy towards others. If you dislike someone or wish that they would act in a different way towards you, then try changing the way you think about them. Picture them smiling at you and being as you had hoped. You will soon begin to see the results, as others develop a more positive attitude to you and the things you want start to come to you.

Once you discover the power of thought, you need never be helpless again.

Live In The Present

When you open this book here, it is an opportunity to give yourself a wonderful gift. Let the here and now, this moment in time, have your attention, your energy and your commitment and you will truly be living life to the full.

Most of us are hooked on the past and the future. We go over the past, wishing to bring it back, believing it was better than the present or wondering what would have happened if we'd done things differently. We think about the future, plotting, planning, investing in it and believing that it will be better, more interesting and more satisfying than the present.

Check out what you are doing right now. Are you trying to recapture what is already past or rushing ahead to tomorrow, wishing your life away? Are you trying to solve something that hasn't yet happened or undo something which has? Are you trying to avoid today's responsibilities? It isn't going to work if this is your motivation. Today you need to deal with today. The truth is that we can only ever exist in this moment in time. In another moment, right now it has become the past and the moment to come is still the future. We can change neither the past nor the future, but we have complete power in the present, although mostly we don't realise it.

Living in the past and the future is the way we choose to distract ourselves from living in the present. We allow the present to be a blur, a rush, a muddle. We exist in it but we don't live in it. Our concentration and energy is elsewhere. And this is a tragedy, because when we do this we never live fully. Life is something we get through or wish away, rather than savour, feel, enjoy and appreciate. It's like gulping a fast-food meal when you could be lingering over a wonderful banquet.

Give yourself the gift of today. Let today be everything. Whether it is sad or happy, frustrating or a joy, feel it to the full. Breathe deeply and be present in your body. Look at the people around you and see who they really are. Make today's decisions and leave tomorrow's for tomorrow, and then let today be the best it can possibly be. Choose to give yourself and those around you pleasure. Trust that when you live in today the past and the future will take care of themselves beautifully, without unnecessary attention from you.

Know that you have everything you need right here, right now, today.

Grieving

When you open this book here, know that this is a time for grieving. It is a time for sadness and sorrow, and only when you deal with this will you be free to move on in your life.

Are you losing someone very important in your life through some kind of separation? Or perhaps they have left already and now you are dealing with the aftermath? Is something very important to you coming to an end? The life you have lived may be changing, and although you may be going on to better and brighter times, it is still natural to grieve for the people, places or events that you are moving away from.

Or is it your dreams which have not come to fruition? Have you been badly let down and left with the need to grieve for the dream of what you once had or thought that you were going to have? Grieving for your dreams can be an especially painful kind of grief because the evidence of the loss is less tangible. The grief is about what you didn't have, rather than what you had and then lost.

There is a huge array of circumstances that can cause you intense grief, leaving you with a sense of a deep and painful loss. Often, however, you may find that your grief gets glossed over or trivialised. Don't let others define what you need to grieve over. Respect your own feelings and follow your heart.

Do not avoid your grief, as any grieving left uncompleted will always be there. You will carry it forward and it will be influencing your current experiences and transactions right now. If you want to be free of it, you'll have to face your feelings. But be reassured that the more deeply you grieve, the sooner your grief will pass.

If you are not aware of feeling grief in your life at the moment, know that this is asking you to recognise that it is around and influencing you. If you are unsure as to what it is that you need to grieve for, now is the time to dig a little deeper and find what it was that wasn't properly grieved for at the time. The answer is always there.

When you grieve, you need to go through the process of facing how painful the loss really is to you, and you need to feel the anger at losing what it is that you have cherished. You need to feel and experience the pain of your loss and only then will you come through to the relief of acceptance and full healing. None of these stages can be skipped over or ignored if you really want to be free of your grief.

Beneath your grief, joy is buried. Deal with the grief and the joy will shine through and fill your life with new hope and possibilities.

Health

When you open this book here, it is time to be aware of your physical health and its importance for your well-being and happiness. There is a saying which goes, 'He who has health has hope, he who has hope has everything'. To stay healthy is to look after yourself physically, emotionally and spiritually, to give yourself what you need, to notice and act on the signs when something is wrong and to address the problem. Know that if you have personality traits, characteristics or life experiences which leave you feeling unhappy or uncomfortable, then you are out of balance in one of these areas. You will only have true health when you address the fears, unmet needs and unresolved emotions in your life.

It is important to eat good food, to get enough sleep and to use your body physically. Take the time to fit these things into your life. Avoid chemicals, drugs and processed foods. Take regular exercise that you enjoy, and create a sense of safety and comfort in the room where you sleep.

All these are vital, but there is far more to genuine good health. All injury and illness is created by what is going on in our lives, and by our feelings. When your body is hurt or sick, it is trying to tell you something. Treat the illness or injury on the surface, but listen to the underlying message too. If you don't do this, you will attract the same problem again, for your body is the physical manifestation of your personality.

Look at what may be behind any ill health that you have. Do you need to slow down and rest more? Are you shouldering too many burdens or doing back-breaking work? Is there something you can't stomach or which is making you sick? What is proving difficult to handle? What can't you face? Or are you being inflexible, stiff-necked and stubborn about something? Trust your own instinct about what is going on and begin to change whatever is not working in your life. As your feelings of anxiety, pressure, fear, worry or anger disappear, so will your bad health.

Support good health by taking responsibility for it and going to practitioners who treat the root causes as well as the surface symptoms. Don't put up with being dismissed or belittled. Know that you are your own best healer and the best judge of what you need. Create laughter and fun in your life – they are the best healers of all.

Good health is possible no matter how much illness or injury you have suffered. Believe that you can be as well and as healthy as you want to be, and fill your life with joy.

Consequences

When you open this book here, it is time to address the issue of consequences. A consequence is the result or the effect of something which has already happened. We tend mostly to associate consequences with outcomes that are unpleasant or unwelcome, but it is important to recognise that consequences can be wonderful and enriching too.

What are you dealing with that demands that you think carefully about what the true consequences will be? What is in your life right now that you are not recognising, or is there as the result of the way you have behaved, acted or thought earlier? If you feel like an innocent victim, you need to know that you have been a part of the events that have led you to this point. The way that you handle things from here on in will create further consequences. You need to stop and assess how you got to this place and determine the best way forward.

Consequences are about not putting your head in the sand like the proverbial ostrich. They are about being clear, honest and far-sighted about what went before and what will result ahead. They demand that you recognise your power in your own life and deal with it. Are you avoiding looking at the consequences of what is around at the moment? Are you willing to see your role in all of this?

Consequences are about taking responsibility, being willing to face up to the fact that everything that you do and don't do has an effect. You make a choice, you act in a certain way, there is a certain outcome. You make a different choice, you act in a different way, there is a different outcome. Everything that we do or fail to do has a consequence. Now is the time to look at your part in your own life. You may find that you are proud and satisfied – or maybe you need to acknowledge that you'll have to make changes in order for the outcome to change.

Make conscious choices which are constructive and you can anticipate and appreciate the positive consequences.

The Only Way Out
Is Through

When you open this book here, be proud of yourself and know that it is safe to trust that all will be well. You are on the right path and you have the courage to follow it and reach the outcome you want.

When we are faced with something painful, difficult or demanding, it is tempting to look for a shortcut, a way around or a way out. We don't want to have feelings which hurt or are uncomfortable and we don't want to dwell on painful events or do things which are tough.

But the truth is that shortcuts and avoidance tactics never work. When we try these, we only end up back in the same place we started from or somewhere equally bad. Our path is going to be blocked until we face the same challenges again and this time accept the experience and go through it.

The way out of any difficulty or painful event is to go through it, eyes wide open, with acceptance and love, even if you don't know where it's going to lead. It's about facing up to what needs to be faced, accepting what needs accepting and being willing to stick with something and see it through. Just keep putting one foot in front of the other. In this way, you will emerge the other side of it all, stronger and wiser and with no need to face that experience again. You will come out in a different place, emotionally and spiritually, to the one you started from. You will have gained vital understanding and awareness which will be of lasting value to you.

Whatever you are facing or going through right now, know that it came into your life to bring you valuable experience and to teach you things you need to know for the next steps on your life's path. Don't resist or fight it and stop trying to figure out a way to carry on while avoiding it, for if you do this, you'll only create more pain for yourself.

Instead, trust that no matter how hard it feels now, you can go through this and it will come to an end sooner than you think. Follow the darkness and the light will appear. There is resolution and peace ahead for you, so go forward with joy in your heart and know that you will never be given more to deal with than you can manage. You are safe.

Gift

When you open this book here, let yourself feel optimistic. Something of benefit is entering your life around this time.

Maybe someone is about to give you an object or possession that will bring you pleasure, joy and satisfaction. Perhaps you are about to receive money, a win of some sort, or something is going to be cheaper than you expected. Be sure to appreciate it, no matter how big or small it may be, because through appreciation we open the door for further gifts.

Maybe your gift won't be as obvious as something which comes gift-wrapped. You may be about to receive a kindness or thoughtful act which will lift your heart and enrich your life. Remember that when people put themselves out for you, they provide you with the gift of their energy and goodwill. Never take this for granted. This is the true currency of this world. Material goods carry and symbolise this energy while actions and love embody it.

If you are struggling right now, you may be hard pushed to find the gift in your life or to believe that one is just around the corner. Sometimes the gift to yourself is to find the benefit in your experience. This is what you need to do now. What good will come from what you are going through? What lessons can be learnt? What gift will come into your life through dealing with a challenge presenting itself now? How can this take you on to a new path or in a different direction to the one that you anticipated? What are you being freed up for that you did not anticipate or even desire?

Know that you will look back and appreciate this with the benefit of hindsight, so you may as well enjoy it now. There is something much better waiting for you and all of this is to make sure that you are available for it.

Trust that forces are guiding you. That doors close in order to direct you to the right door which will be open to you. But you must be willing to involve yourself fully in the process. You will get what you want if you stick with this.

Know that there is a gift and that there will be a time when you will celebrate. This is a wonderful certainty.

Pleasure and Pain

When you open this book here, it is time to be softer towards yourself and to understand that there is always a good reason for the things that you do. If you are telling yourself that you've got things wrong, or if you are wondering why on earth you did something, know that you did the best you could and stop giving yourself a hard time about it.

Whatever you have done, whatever choices you have made, everything has been done in an effort to give yourself the best possible outcome. All of us follow the same motivation – to seek pleasure and avoid pain. When you understand how we do this, you will be able to make sense of all that you do and all that you have done, and to make new choices.

As children, we tried to win love and approval from those we depended on for survival, and to protect ourselves from physical and emotional pain and injury. If we got hurt, we learned to avoid whatever hurt us. Sometimes we were hurt by those we trusted most and who we were closest to. So we learned not to trust, and to stay away from closeness. If we were repeatedly criticised, we tried not to do the things which provoked the criticism. We did whatever worked to survive with the least pain. We also looked for ways to bring pleasure into our lives in whatever way we could. If something felt good, we pursued it, whether it was truly good for us or not.

As adults, we have often ended up very muddled about what actually causes us pleasure and what causes us pain. We do things which we believe will bring pleasure into our lives, such as eating, drinking, spending money, but we do them to excess and end up creating pain. Sometimes we develop habits and ways of living to cover up our painful feelings. Or we avoid those things which demand effort and responsibility, seeing these as potentially painful activities, when in fact their benefits would bring us enormous pleasure.

What do you consider causes pleasure or pain in your life? Maybe it's time to re-evaluate. What ideas do you carry from your childhood which are no longer relevant or appropriate?

Know that you have been doing the best that you could up until now. Be proud of yourself and give yourself the love and approval you deserve. Then you can begin to make choices which will minimise pain and bring real pleasure into your life.

Take risks, be bold, ask for what you want. Know that it is enough just to be you and that to be respectful, honest and clear will always bring you the best possible outcome.

Getting Stuck

When you open this book here, it is to acknowledge that you have reached an impasse. Your progress is being blocked in this situation and you need to stop and address this now.

Are you finding yourself pushing water uphill, with everything taking up a lot more of your energy than you anticipated? Did you expect to be further along or even finished with this by now? Do you have a sense of going around in circles? Do you feel that you are making headway, only to find yourself right back where you started? If the answer to any or all of these questions is yes, then now is the time to admit that you are stuck and to pause and address the situation from a different perspective.

Sometimes humans are like flies. When they try to get something or somewhere and their efforts fail to produce the expected results, they often just carry on doing exactly what they did before, only harder. Have you watched a fly wear itself out, banging against a window which is closed? It knows where it wants to get to, and it will not accept that it is stuck because it cannot see what is holding it back. Even when another open window is close to hand, it may never find this alternative because it does not have the capacity to accept that what it is doing isn't working.

You have a huge advantage over that fly. You can stop, sit down on the window ledge and admit that despite your best efforts something unseen is blocking your path. It can be scary to do this. It takes courage, but it is the only way to move forward in any real sense of the word.

How many times have you attempted to surmount the insurmountable? How many different approaches have you taken to sorting out the same problems, trying to accomplish a dream, or getting the better of an addiction or neurosis? What you need to know is that you cannot do it alone. And you cannot do it this way. It is not working.

What works is admitting that you are powerless. This is where your real power lies. You need to step back and let a force greater than yourself guide you to the open window, to the path that you cannot see right now and so do not know about. You need to give up trying to push forward. Brute strength and determination will not suffice on this occasion. Let the universal wisdom guide you. Contact your own spirituality and then put your energy into something else for a while.

Just for today, accept that everything is exactly as it is and let go. The answer will come, the block will clear. While respecting yourself and keeping yourself safe, now is the time for the path of least resistance. It does work.

Self-Respect

When you open this book here, it is to remind you that the foundation stone of a happy and fulfilled life is self-respect.

To show respect means to give attention and consideration and to look after the details. When you respect yourself, you care for yourself in every way. You nurture your body and give it enough good food and sleep. You exercise your mind, you develop your opinions and know that they matter and that you have a right to be heard. You learn to like yourself for who you are, not for the things that you achieve or what you could become. You notice the goodwill and energy you put into things, your talents and what you give to others. And then you appreciate yourself for all of those things.

With healthy self-respect, you no longer depend on the approval of others for a sense of well-being. And you are able to make clear, healthy decisions. You like and approve of yourself and find your own company a pleasure. Your relationships with others become far more satisfying, because you aren't looking to others to make you feel whole, or to make you feel better. You can do that on your own. And with self-respect, you never let yourself be treated badly or put down. You speak up for yourself and walk away from those who don't value you or don't behave well towards you.

If you are low on self-respect, then know that it is up to you to develop and strengthen it. Look at the beliefs you have which keep you feeling bad about yourself. Toss them out and replace them with positive beliefs. Use affirmations – positive statements – as a way to change your beliefs. Repeat them to yourself hundreds of times a day until they become your truth. Explore your childhood pains and heal the hurts that ate away at your self-respect or failed to help you develop it.

Don't stay around people who put you down or hurt you. Seek out those who have respect and goodwill for you. Treat yourself in the way that they treat you, with compassion and tenderness.

With healthy self-respect, you will flourish and blossom. You will see yourself for the unique, special and wonderful being that you are.

You Get What You Need

W hen you open this book here, it is to remind you that in life you always get what you need before you get what you want.

It's easy to believe that you know what you need for your life to progress as you want it to. Most of us wish for things to go as we have planned or dreamed. We wish to control the way events unfold, so that pleasure is maximised and struggle and hardship can be avoided. We take this approach around the big issues, such as life and death, relationships, our career, homes and money, as well as around the little issues – whether something happens on time or as planned, for example.

But the greater forces beyond our knowing often have a view of how life is meant to be which is very different to our own.

You are on a journey where you are forever being encouraged to learn and grow. This is the purpose of your life and the reason that you are here. If everything always went according to your own plan, life would only be easy, pleasurable and straightforward and there is very little growth in that. It is when times are hardest that we do our growing at the level of the personality and the soul, because this is when we have to turn inwards. This is when we get to know and understand more about ourselves and discover our true potential and resources.

Are things not as you wish them to be right now? Do you find yourself asking, Why me, why this, why now? If you do, then be reassured. There is an important learning to be had which in time will show itself.

Maybe things are being slowed down because the timing isn't right. Maybe you are being directed on to a different path altogether. It's easy to cling on to something that you're sure you want without realising that something better is just around the next corner. Maybe you are about to discover new levels of inner strength and fortitude through what is presenting in your life at the moment. You will come through this situation with a greater sense of confidence, combined with a sense of humility. We get what we need before we get what we want because we need to learn that we are not the only force in control of our destiny. A force greater than yourself is guiding you towards the best possible outcome.

Now is the time for trusting and going with the flow. Develop a positive attitude, welcome it into your life and learn from it.

Denial

When you open this book here, know that there is something which you are denying or not facing up to, and which you need to face if you are to move forward in the way you would like.

Denial is what is going on when you tell yourself that something true isn't true, or that it doesn't really matter or doesn't even exist. Often we can use it so effectively that we don't even remember the event or feeling we are suppressing. We come to believe that whatever happened or whatever we felt never even occurred, and we get good at convincing ourselves and others of this. Or we can acknowledge the issue, but tell ourselves that it wasn't really painful or damaging. By doing this, we deny ourselves the opportunity to have the appropriate feelings that would heal the hurt. Sometimes what is denied is a single event, and other times we deny whole areas of our lives or feelings. People who say that they had perfect childhoods, that they don't feel anger or fear, or who deny problems which are obvious to outsiders, are in denial.

The trouble with denial is that it doesn't work and it leads to all kinds of painful results. Denial can make you reckless and thoughtless. In denial, people take foolish risks or avoid facing their problems. Even more importantly, whatever it is you are denying will make a bigger and bigger negative impact on your life until you face it and acknowledge it. It gets worse, not better. You can't be open, honest and fulfilled if you are in denial about a part of your life or a part of who you are. And to admit something to yourself while continuing to deny it to other people won't work either. For doing this doesn't allow you to truly be yourself.

When you are in denial, you are likely to repeat painful patterns in relationships and be surprised when things keep on failing to work out as you hoped. You keep trying to fix or solve problems in your life which can never be properly resolved until you break your denial and deal with the underlying issues.

Now is the time for you to come out of denial and choose to be someone who has nothing to hide. Let yourself remember hidden secrets, buried pain, frightening events and painful feelings. When they're out in the open, their power over you will begin to diminish. When you let go of denial, you become free, you become braver and wiser. Your life will begin to make more sense, both your past and your future.

Denial is like a blanket of fear which covers everything it touches. Dare to lift the blanket, to see clearly and breathe more easily, and you'll feel the freedom.

Angels

When you open this book here, be happy and know that all is well, because you are supported and protected by Angels. Angels are the bridge between us and the divine and as such are a power unto themselves. Although we don't often see them, Angels are everywhere. Angels are all around us and are always ready to bring their powerful healing energy to us.

Whether you see them or not, and whether you believe in them or not, know that Angels are here with you now and are ready to help. Angels are able to direct the unlimited positive energy of the universe towards specific areas and issues. When things are good, they are around you helping to make them even better, and they can help you to sort out whatever is troubling or puzzling you. They can point you in the right direction and support you through both the wonderful and the tougher parts of your journey. The closer you move towards a more spiritual life, the more easily you will be able to connect with the Angels.

Are you having a painful or difficult time right now? Do you feel stuck, uncertain or helpless? Is your energy low? Are you struggling to keep going with something – or to let go of it — whether it is a job, a relationship or a task you've set yourself?

If so, you can make it easier on yourself by asking the Angels to help you. You don't have to be a believer to ask and receive. They are waiting for you to ask, as they can only involve themselves by invitation. So, go ahead, tell them what you need and then relax and trust. The signs of their presence will be all around you, and when you know how to spot them you will feel comforted and reassured that a greater power is there to help you.

Angel signs take many forms. A white feather, a rainbow in a patch of oil, noticing a small statue or a picture of an Angel — all these let you know that Angels are near. And there will be inner signs too. Decisions will become easier, your choices clearer, your determination stronger and your outlook more positive.

Accept help and love from the Angels and you will never feel alone again.

What You Focus On Grows

W hen you open this book here, it is to assure you that you create your own reality and direct your own destiny. Where you put your focus has immeasurable influence on how your life unfolds, because your focus is made up of your energy and expectations and these are the tools with which you shape your life.

If life is going as you wish it to, then you are focusing on the elements and ideals that work for you. As long as you continue to do this, your life will go on developing and flourishing in this way. Be excited, be inspired. If there is something more that you want, put your energy and focus on to the outcome that you desire and watch it continue to grow and develop in your life.

If you don't know how to realise your dreams or draw the events or experiences that you desire into your life, then you need to learn to focus on your ideals. Make a collage of magazine pictures that best represent what you want and look at it every day. Write about it, talk about it but avoid worrying about it. Because if you worry, what you focus on will grow!

Take stock of how things have been developing recently. Are things going the way that you wish them to, or in the opposite direction? You need to know that whatever is manifesting in your life right now is there because you have focused on it. Only by understanding this will you have the power to uncreate it or create something better.

If things are bad, stop and review how much of your focus you have put into just this outcome. Remember the universe can't work in negatives. If we tell someone not to picture a ripe, juicy orange, they can't do anything other than picture it. Well, it is the same for universal law. If you say that you don't want to be abandoned or broke or jobless, all the universe gets is these images. Naturally, it concludes that these are the things that you have in mind for yourself and it does its best to help you create them in your life. Of course, if instead you were to declare that you want to be loved, professionally fulfilled and financially secure it will work equally hard to help you gain these elements!

Universal law does not discriminate. It is not its role to question what you focus on. But you must discriminate, because what you focus on grows and grows. Start now and see what you really want flourishing in your life.

Confrontation

When you open this book here, it is because there is the need to deal with something in an honest and upfront manner.

Confrontation is the opposite of avoidance. It is about saying what needs to be said and admitting that there are issues to be dealt with. Has someone recently challenged you about something in a way which does not allow either of you to avoid what needs to be faced? Or perhaps it is you who needs to challenge another?

Whichever way round it is, know that confrontation is healthy and life-affirming, but that it should take place in a manner which is respectful and safe. If one of you is screaming down the telephone, acting unpleasantly or refusing to speak, then this is actually a way of avoiding confrontation. Instead, you are simply dumping on one another.

Healthy confrontation requires that the person doing the confronting is straightforward, calm and clear about what it is they wish to say. Sometimes, if you feel unsafe or if you feel unable to face the person that you need to confront, it is best to do so by letter. And make sure that you do it yourself. You won't reap the benefits if you get someone else to do it for you.

What is it that you need to deal with through confrontation at the moment? Is there something that you are avoiding admitting because you are scared of the consequences? Who or what do you need to tackle? Do you feel that someone else has the key to your happiness? Know that until you deal with it, it will always hold you back. Running away from it only means that it will present itself once again to you somewhere up ahead.

Confrontation requires being willing to state who you are and what you believe in. It means being willing to define yourself regardless of what others want of you or how they judge you. It's about being willing to deal with the issue even if others around you avoid it or refuse to face it. It is one of the most liberating acts available to you and only when you have mastered it are you really free to be an adult. And remember that it demands honesty. For if you only say what feels comfortable, you are hemmed in by the truths that you did not tell.

Know that it is important to respect others, and that right now it is most important to respect yourself. You can do it. See it as a gift to yourself.

Joy

When you open this book here, know that you are blessed and fortunate because an abundance of joy is coming into your life.

If you have been going through hard times and feeling pain, sorrow, grief, worry or fear, then be assured that this is coming to an end and a period of pleasure and gladness is coming to you. Just as the sun rises each morning and light follows darkness, so it is with our emotions. After pain and sadness, there will always be an opportunity for joy and laughter.

Both pain and joy are necessary in the balance of life. Be sure that you do not reject either of them. Don't think of hurt, anger and sadness as bad and of joy as good – it is better to simply let all emotions come and go without judging them. If you did not feel anger, sadness and fear, then you would not feel joy either. They are opposite sides of the same coin.

Be aware of the joy, or the opportunity for joy, that is all around you. Don't turn away from it or dismiss it. There is joy to be found in small things as well as big ones, and it is important to open yourself to it and allow it into your heart. Hear the joy in a child's laughter, see the funny side of mishaps, appreciate the people around you who love you – and the ways in which they show this – and you will become a channel for joy.

Most of all, find the joy inside of you. Reach inside for the child waiting there and take him or her on an outing with you. See things with a child's wonder, take in the beauty which is within your reach, laugh when something is funny or silly. Children have an enormous capacity for joy which so often is stifled when we reach adulthood. But however crushed joy is, it will never go away. All you have to do is dust off the cobwebs, set aside your anxiety and unleash your wonderful joyousness. Even if to start with you can only take tiny steps.

The more you do this, the more your health will flourish and the more successful you will be. Smile at those around you and you change the atmosphere instantly. And once you are giving out joy you will receive it back in ever larger quantities.

Judging

When you open this book here, it is because you are judging either yourself or others in a critical or negative way or failing to make a judgement that needs to be made.

To judge is to form an opinion based on all of the information available, in order to make a good decision or form a fair point of view. When we get stuck and we don't know what to do next to accomplish our goals or make the changes we wish for, it is often because we fear the consequences of making a judgement. Remember that an honest judgement is simply your own opinion at this moment in time and that you are entitled to this. Don't jump to rash conclusions and don't assume that others will agree with you. But do accept that until you know what you really think or want you will keep yourself immobilised or going around in circles. Every judgement has a knock-on effect and you need to be brave enough to deal with this, whatever it is.

Sometimes we are not equipped to make a good judgement, as we do not have enough information. If this is the case then it is better to avoid making a judgement until you do have more information. If you are judging others harshly then maybe it would be best to focus on yourself instead and leave them to be who they are. When we judge too much from a critical place this gets in the way of us achieving our goals and getting what we deserve. For when we make ourselves superior then our judgements will be flawed and we will not benefit from them. If you are in the habit of judging yourself and others negatively at the moment, then it is time to stop. This type of judging takes an awful lot of energy and when you stop you will be able to use this same energy in more constructive, positive ways. You will soon feel the relief of letting go.

If things are going well right now then resist any judgements that you don't deserve this as these are simply based on fear or low self-esteem. Also resist judgements that you are luckier, cleverer or wiser than anyone else, as these are based on arrogance. Instead enjoy your good fortune and wish others well.

If you are having a hard time, facing tough decisions or resisting a move, you need to know that you are a good person with many brave and wise qualities, that you are doing your best and that everything is happening in just the right way. Consult people you trust, make decisions and act for your own good while respecting those around you.

Be kind, decent and fair with yourself and others and know that any judgements made in this light will lead you in the right direction.

Change

W hen you open this book here, it is because you are in the process of change in your life. It is a time of moving forward, even if you are not yet aware of this.

Life is constantly undergoing transformations as you move forward along your path. But sometimes this is more apparent than usual.

Are you involved in something that requires a great deal of upheaval at the moment? Know that you will soon reap the benefits, and the effort involved will be rewarded. Remember that change is stressful and exhausting and be sure to look after yourself properly during this time. Eat well, get lots of sleep and make time to be with yourself. Get some fresh air and spend time connecting with nature, as this is an effective way of refuelling your depleted energy reserves.

Or are the changes that you are experiencing not sufficiently obvious for you to realise that change is the issue to hand? Perhaps you want to convince yourself that something is more permanent than it really is. Don't worry if this is the case. You will be able to admit the fact that this is only temporary when you are good and ready, but in the meantime don't commit yourself to anything that can't be easily undone.

Change can seem like chaos and confusion. Do not despair if this is what surrounds you. You are in the white water of the wave that has broken and beneath the surface the next one is forming. Trust the process. If you resist and try to recapture the wave that has already broken, you will only slow down the new one. Something new is forming in your life. Something bright is up ahead and you will find what you want in it. Remember not to hold on too tightly to what you do have. There needs to be room for change in your life. When you allow little changes often, you will find that the big changes don't have to be so big any more.

If you are not experiencing change in your life right now, then you opened this book here to be directed towards change. Is it time for you to actively make changes? Would you like to do this on an internal or external level? What would you like to change? We live in a world which is filled with tools to make changes. Investigate your options. Get honest about what really matters to you. What would make a significant difference? Do you need to stand up to someone, sort yourself out, or try to make an impact on the world you live in? Only you will know in your heart what it is that you need to change.

Welcome change and let its blessings into your life.

Sharing

When you open this book here, it is to remind you of the importance of sharing. To share is to give some of what one has to others. It can mean sharing your possessions, or it can mean opening up inwardly and sharing your thoughts and feelings by talking about and demonstrating them.

Learning to share, both materially and emotionally, is a life skill which is vital to happiness. The opposite of sharing is withholding, which means keeping what you have to yourself. Those who withhold their possessions, their thoughts or their feelings soon begin to feel isolated, lonely, misunderstood and unloved. While those who learn to share and do so with goodwill and generosity will always feel connected to and loved by others.

Some of us never learned to share as children because our parents didn't teach us how. Perhaps we learned to share our possessions but not our inner world. If our parents kept everything to themselves, we will have learned to do the same. Or we may have been ridiculed and put down by others for sharing who we are, for telling them what we thought or felt, and so decided it was safer to keep it all inside.

If this was your experience, then you may have grown up wary of sharing, afraid that you will be belittled for showing more of who you are. It will take courage to change this pattern, but it is vital that you do. Your courage will bring wonderful results. The most successful way to come close to another person is to reach out and tell them what is really going on for you, while at the same time allowing them to tell you what is going on for them. In this way, sharing becomes the tool through which you express yourself and know others. And it's through sharing that you'll find the support you need for dealing with your issue. Once we share, miracles can happen.

What is it you are not sharing? Who are you afraid to share with? Be brave, decide to give generously of yourself, and you'll soon reap the rewards.

Protection

When you open this book here, know that you need to address the issue of protection in your life.

Are you taking unnecessary risks without paying appropriate attention to the consequences? Are you safe enough in your own environment or in the outside world? Are you properly defending yourself from trouble or harm?

This does not ask you to become neurotic or to panic, but it does ask you to address the more obvious ways in which you keep yourself safe. Are you looking after yourself physically? Do you have appropriate boundaries around your body and your physical possessions? Who is looking after your money? Don't take things for granted. Question your old habits, review your arrangements, admit to any lingering concerns and deal with them now.

You also need to protect yourself emotionally. Where do you begin and end? Who is sapping your energy and wearing you out? Protect yourself by looking after yourself properly. Speak up or walk away if someone is treating you unfairly. Judge carefully who to trust. Gather information about someone, do not just rush in to any kind of involvement until you have done this. Check out people and circumstances before committing yourself. Be careful about how much you reveal of yourself, and to whom.

You can create your own protection by surrounding yourself in a bubble of white light. Imagine drawing the light up all around you. Start from the ground, front and back, totally surrounding yourself. Then twist the light over your head and bring it back down again, sealing it where it meets the ground. This simple act will contain you and your energy and help to protect you from the negative energy of others and from having others drain your energy. The more you practise visualising this, the more powerful it will become. You can experiment with your own colours or shapes. Some people like to use pyramids and strong, bright colours. Use this method to protect yourself, your loved ones and your possessions.

Remember too, that the spirits and the Angels watch over us and protect us. Those that we knew who have gone before us also safeguard us and lead us towards the optimum path. But you need to listen to the whispers, your gut instincts and your intuition as this is how their messages come to you. The more you tune into the subtle messages, the greater protection you can provide for yourself. And when you are protected you will be better able to make decisions and accomplish your goals.

Treasures

When you open this book here, it is to draw your attention to all of the wonderful things in your life and in the world around you.

Are you full of appreciation for what you have right now? Make sure that you don't take any of it for granted, or become used to it so quickly that you fail to remember how much good there is in your life.

If you're unsure about something, or are faced with a dilemma, now is the time to stop and really focus on the good in what is going on around you. There is always some good in everything. And when you find this, it will lead you on to the right path.

If you cannot find anything to appreciate at the moment, then focus on the little things. Thank the universe for providing us with miracles every day. Look at a new-born baby or a bird, look at the vastness of the sky, appreciate the constant beating of your heart and your body's innate ability to go on following each breath with the next. Know that your time on earth is infinitely precious, even when it is challenging.

When you stop appreciating, you become sour and despondent.

When you fail to appreciate the treasures in your life, it is time to admit that you are in pain. When you cannot find room for joy, it is because you are not allowing room for your sadness, anger or grief. Let these feelings out now and appreciate them too as an important part of the whole picture. Because once they are properly expressed, you will be able to see the beauty that was there all along.

Make time to stop and appreciate people too. Treasure their uniqueness and treat them as you would treat something very precious to you. Never underestimate the importance of your fellow souls in life's journey. And most importantly, treasure yourself. The way others treat you will be equal to the way you treat yourself. If you want to change anything, this is where to start.

Do you know how important you are? Do you know how wonderful, unique and precious you are? Your essence is as pure and as perfect as an unblemished jewel. You are priceless in your rarity and uniqueness and the universal force values you as highly as everyone else. Now it is time for you to treasure yourself too.

Decisions

When you open this book here, know that the time is right for you to make a decision, or that it soon will be. You are going to have to make up your mind.

Do you feel relieved at the prospect, or resistant and defensive? Do you know what the decision is about, or are you confused by the idea that a decision is required on your part?

Sometimes making a decision can be instantaneous. We have already gathered all that we need to know, and we just have to be brave enough to admit what it is that we have decided and face the consequences, good, bad or a mix of the two.

Other times, decision-making is a slow and laborious task and it is best to acknowledge this and work with it. The more you become conscious of how you go about making decisions, the easier your decision-making will become. You will know how to support yourself, and become clearer about what does and doesn't work for you.

In order to come to a decision, you have to come to a conclusion using the evidence to hand. It is important to involve all parts of yourself when gathering this evidence. Review the facts that you have, and check if you need more information before you can proceed. Also, consider how you feel about this because feelings are very important. Next, consider your instinct. What do you feel in your gut, even if you have no rational evidence to support this? Know that your gut will know more than you. Your unconscious has more information than you can ever hold in your conscious mind at any one time. Trust your instincts because they promote your best interests.

A useful trick is to flip a coin to help in the decision-making process. You don't actually have to follow the result, just pretend to yourself that you will for a little while and see how it feels. Then reverse the process and see how that feels. It leaves you better informed.

Be assured that decisions are the gateways to your future. Avoiding them only keeps you where you already are or leaves the decision up to outside forces that you may not appreciate. And indecisiveness is the greatest known cause of stress. If you are really stuck, ask to be guided from above. Ask that one choice may shine more brightly or that all the doors will be closed except for the right one. The Angels are happy to help you make decisions, but they cannot help unless you request it.

Finally, always know that every decision is the right decision to take you where you are meant to go.

Everything Is As It Should Be

When you open this book here, be comforted and reassured by the knowledge that whatever is happening in your life right now is exactly the way it should be in order to bring you the best possible long-term outcome.

If good things are coming to you and you are feeling happy, appreciated and loved, then know that you deserve all that you have and let yourself enjoy it to the full. Let go of any guilt or unworthy feelings that threaten to spoil your pleasure and trust that you have been given exactly what you should have.

But if you are going through hardship, pain, grief, or doubt, then you may feel that life is cruel and that what is happening to you is unfair and unnecessary.

In fact, the tough times we go through are as important as the easy, happy times. It is when life seems tough that we learn the most important lessons about ourselves and our ability to cope. Our painful experiences help to shape us and give us depth and understanding. If you can come through them and out the other side, you will be stronger, wiser and richer in spirit.

Life is never all hard times or all pleasurable ones. It's a mixture of both because each then balances the other. Neither will last indefinitely, but each will shine light on the other and help you to appreciate the value it brings you.

If things are hard for you, then recognise that that's the way you need them to be right now, even if the value of what you're going through isn't yet clear. And if you stop and ask yourself what the benefits of your situation are, they may be clearer than you think. You do know what you need to do in order to handle whatever is presenting in your life right now. Don't waste time on regrets as everything has been structured to bring you to this moment.

When you accept that everything is exactly as it should be, then you can stop struggling for solutions or quick fixes. Instead, take a deep breath and relax, knowing that events will unfold in the best way possible and that easier times are ahead.

Live in the moment, for you do not know the outcome of all of this, even though you may think that you do. Stop focusing on the future or regretting the past, everything is as it should be.

Childhood Issues

When you open this book here, it is because whatever is going on in your life right now is being influenced by unresolved issues from your past which you need to look at and deal with.

Often when childhood pain and sadness have been buried deep inside us they affect our behaviour as adults, without us even being aware of what's going on. We operate, some or all of the time, in a childlike way, seeing ourselves as powerless and dependent on the moods or choices of others. This was true when we were children, and because of this, even as adults, certain behaviour in others can trigger the same reaction in us now. Sometimes we get caught up in acting out who we think we should be because we don't really know who we are. So we oscillate between pretending to be a competent adult and being like a child, out of our depth.

It takes courage to recognise that this is what is happening, but there are lots of clues to follow up if you are willing to use them. Is your reaction out of proportion to what is going on around you? Are you more angry, sad or hurt than seems appropriate? Do you feel helpless and dependent on others emotionally? Do you tell yourself you shouldn't have certain feelings, or do you try to adjust your moods to fit in with others? Do you spend a great deal of energy trying to please others and then feel resentful that people aren't working as hard to please you?

If this is you, then take time to go back over the past and acknowledge what really happened to you when you were a child. Write a journal of your memories and feelings. Look at photographs, talk to trustworthy people who remember you as a child. Look deep inside yourself for your own truth and for the feelings you had then. If your childhood was painful and difficult, if you were badly treated, hurt or abandoned in any way, then comfort yourself now. Know that you did a great job of surviving and coping. Talk to friends about it and go to a counsellor or therapist for support. Learn that rather than trying to grow up more as adults, sometimes we have to retrace our childhood and start to grow up from there.

By acknowledging the truth of your childhood, and giving it the importance and respect it deserves, you will free yourself to move forward. Then you can be a true adult now, able to react and make choices in response to what is in your life, rather than what once was.

Heal the past and you will heal the present and the future too.

Pressures

When you open this book here, it is because you are feeling under pressure in some area of your life and need to address this before you can move forward.

Pressures are created when you feel troubled, burdened and constrained by people or events. Pressures create stress, which is a feeling that too much is being demanded of your physical or mental energy. When you feel stressed, you are usually overwhelmed, worried, tense and unable to rest, relax or concentrate properly.

If this is happening to you, then you need to look first at what is creating the pressure and whether it is appropriate to change the situation. Is something being demanded of you which you feel unable to give? Have you promised more than you can deliver? Are you taking on responsibilities unnecessarily? If so, then be willing to let go of whatever feels too much. Extend a deadline, hand over tasks to others, do whatever is needed. If you tell yourself that you are indispensable, remember that no one is, and that if you carry on with too much pressure you will simply become ill or injure yourself as a way of escaping from it.

Then look at the demands that you put upon yourself. We

create the greatest pressure inside ourselves. It is often little to do with the outside world and more about how we talk to ourselves. Look at what you expect of yourself and understand that it is time to ease up and be kinder now. Find ways to relieve some of the pressure in a practical way. Write a list instead of carrying it all around in your head. Get the tasks which are creating the most stress finished. Then admit that you are not going to tackle some matters now, fix a date for dealing with them in future and let go of it all until then. If it helps, break a task up into small steps and only concentrate on the step in hand. Remember that a journey of a thousand miles begins with just one step, but must be followed by the second one after the first. You can do it, one step at a time.

Know that most of the activity which creates pressure and stress is simply a way of avoiding the feelings which you will have if you stop and rest more often. Listen to your nurturing inner voice instead, the voice of your warm and loving internal carer, which tells you to slow down, rest and find peace.

Recognise pressures for the distraction that they are, and let them go. Change your pace and let the quality of your life improve beyond imagination.